I could go for something

JELL-O ®

BRAND

I could go for something

I could go for something

JELL-O®

BRAND

Publications International, Ltd.

Favorite Brand Name Recipes at www.fbnr.com

Senior Brand Manager, JELL-O Brands: Lisa Powers
Desserts & Snacks Division Promotion Manager: Carol D. Harris
Kraft Kitchens Consumer Foods Manager: Normajean Longfield
Contributing Writer: Hunter & Associates, Inc.

Photography: Stephen Hamilton Photographics, Inc.
Photographer: Stephen Hamilton
Prop Stylist: Paula Walters
Food Stylists: Donna Coates, Walter Moeller
Assistant Food Stylist: Susie Skoog

Pictured on the front cover *(clockwise from top left):* 5-Minute Chocolate Banana Parfaits *(page 28),* Tropical Cake Squares *(page 80),* Peanut Butter Loaf *(page 68)* and Melon Salad *(page 20).*
Pictured on the back cover: COOL 'N EASY® Pie *(page 60).*

ISBN: 1-4127-2363-9

Manufactured in China

8 7 6 5 4 3 2 1

Preparation/Cooking Times: Preparation times are based on the approximate amount of time required to assemble the recipe before cooking, baking, chilling or serving. These times include preparation steps such as measuring, chopping and mixing. The fact that some preparations and cooking can be done simultaneously is taken into account. Preparation of optional ingredients and serving suggestions is not included.

I could go for something JELL-O® BRAND

I Could Go For Something JELL-O

For more than 100 years, Jell-O has adapted to changes in lifestyles and eating habits—becoming a brand recognized by 99 percent of Americans and used regularly in nearly every home in America. With more than 125 varieties of snacks and desserts that can help make every day just a little sweeter, it's no wonder that Jell-O is "America's Most Famous Dessert™." This year continues the tradition of creating innovative, fun desserts and snacks with another spectacular collection of Jell-O recipes that are sure to please.

The possibilities are endless with gelatin. It can be served plain, combined with fruit and whipped topping in a parfait or concentrated into a fun Jiggler snack. Sparkling Jell-O can be mixed with club soda or tantalize the tongue and create shimmering molds.

The JELL-O team has been busy this year creating new recipes like Juicy Jell-O. Instead of **cold water,** you can now juice up your gelatin with fruit juices like white grape, apple or orange to create a more intense flavor. Juicy gelatin can be prepared in molds, special dessert cups or glasses or served cubed in parfaits. It's a great new way to personalize your favorite gelatin treat!

Pudding offers creamy indulgence for every day. With just two cups of milk, any flavor of instant Jell-O pudding and a quick stir, you can make a homemade snack in only five minutes. Plus, you can mix in marshmallows, cookies, candy or nuts for instant variety. Cooked pudding offers even more indulgence and can be prepared in minutes in popular flavors including Tapioca and Rice Pudding. Pudding is also a wonderful filling for cakes and pies, and a necessity when making pudding snack cups or frozen desserts.

Need to impress friends and family with a wow dessert? Jell-O No Bake Desserts take just 15 minutes with no baking. And in a variety of flavors, these easy-to-make desserts are a great way to dazzle your guests.

Delicious desserts and snacks used to take hours to make, but Jell-O brings you hundreds of ideas and products to make each day just a little sweeter, without spending hours in the kitchen.

On the following pages you'll find a delicious variety of recipes that are sure to answer the call for something sweet. For more information, we invite you to browse through the Jell-O Web site at www.jello.com to find even more ideas. When you can go for something sweet, creamy, fun or festive... remember to go for something Jell-O.

Tips & Techniques

All of the recipes appearing in this publication have been developed and tested by the food professionals in the Kraft Test Kitchens to ensure your success in making them. We also share our JELL-O secrets with you. These foolproof tips, many with step-by-step photos, help you get perfect results every time.

GELATIN

Making JELL-O Brand Gelatin Dessert is easy. Just follow the package directions and the results will be a success.

The basic directions as written below are also on the package:

- Stir 1 cup boiling water into 1 package (4-serving size) gelatin at least 2 minutes until completely dissolved. Stir in 1 cup cold water. Refrigerate 4 hours or until firm. (For an 8-serving size package, use 2 cups boiling water and 2 cups cold water.)

- JELL-O Brand Sugar Free Low Calorie Gelatin Dessert is prepared in the same way. It can be used in many recipes that call for JELL-O Brand Gelatin Dessert.

Some tips for success

- To make a mixture that is clear and uniformly set, be sure the gelatin is completely dissolved in boiling water or other boiling liquid before adding the cold water.

- To double a recipe, just double the amounts of gelatin, liquid and other ingredients used, except salt, vinegar and lemon juice. For these, use 1½ times the amount given in the recipe.

- To store prepared gelatin overnight or longer, cover it before refrigerating to prevent drying. Always store gelatin desserts and molds in the refrigerator.

- Generally, gelatin molds are best served right from the refrigerator. A gelatin mold containing fruit or vegetables can remain at room temperature up to 2 hours. Always keep a gelatin mold containing meat, mayonnaise, ice cream or other dairy products refrigerated until ready to serve. Also, do not let it sit at room temperature longer than 30 minutes. Store any leftover gelatin mold in the refrigerator.

How to Speed Up Refrigerating Time

- Choose the right container. Use a metal bowl or mold rather than glass, plastic or china. Metal chills more quickly and the gelatin will be firm in less time than in glass or plastic bowls.

- Use the speed set (ice cube) method. (Do not use this method if you are going to mold gelatin.) For a 4-serving size package, stir ¾ cup boiling water into gelatin in medium bowl at least 2 minutes until completely dissolved. Mix ½ cup cold water and ice cubes to make 1¼ cups. Add to gelatin, stirring until slightly thickened. Remove any remaining ice. Refrigerate 30 minutes for a soft set or 1 to 1½ hours until firm.

(For an 8-serving size package, use 1½ cups boiling water. Mix 1 cup cold water and ice cubes to make 2½ cups.)

- Use the ice bath method. (This method will speed up the preparation of layered gelatin molds.) Prepare gelatin as directed on package. Place bowl of gelatin in a larger bowl of ice and water. Stir occasionally as mixture chills to ensure even thickening.

- Use the blender method. (This method can be used to make quick and easy layered gelatin desserts.) Place 1 package (4-serving size) gelatin and ¾ cup boiling liquid in blender container; cover. Blend on low speed 30 seconds. Mix ½ cup cold water and ice cubes to make 1¼ cups. Add to gelatin, stirring until partially melted; cover. Blend on low speed 30 seconds. Pour into dessert dishes. Refrigerate at least 30 minutes or until set. The mixture sets with a frothy layer on top and a clear layer on bottom. (Use this method for the 4-serving size package only. The volume of liquid required for an 8-serving size package is too large for most blenders.)

Prepare Jell-O Gelatin as directed in Basic Directions on Jell-O Gelatin Package, replacing <u>cold</u> water with cold fruit juice.

"Juicy JELL-O"	JELL-O Gelatin Flavor	Juice Flavor
Outrageous Orange	orange, lemon *or* lime	orange guava juice
Berry-Bop	strawberry	pineapple orange strawberry
Tutti-Frutti	strawberry banana, cherry *or* mixed fruit	pineapple or pinapple orange banana
Peach Passion	peach, apricot *or* lemon	orange peach mango
Berry Sensation	wild strawberry, raspberry *or* mixed fruit	raspberry kiwi
Sunshine Fun	strawberry kiwi, cranberry raspberry *or* orange	orange
Island Paradise	raspberry *or* peach	tropical fruit
Double Orange Berry	orange	orange strawberry banana
Hawaiian Luau	pineapple, orange *or* lemon	pineapple orange or pineapple orange banana
Krazy Kid Kups	berry blue, cherry *or* watermelon	orange strawberry banana

Gelatin Refrigerating Time Chart

In all recipes, for best results, the gelatin needs to be refrigerated to the proper consistency. Use this chart as a guideline to determine the desired consistency and the approximate refrigerating time.

When a recipe says:	It means gelatin should:	Refrigerating Time:		Gelatin Uses:
		Regular set	Speed set*	
"Refrigerate until syrupy"	Be consistency of thick syrup	1 hour	3 minutes	Glaze for pies, fruit
"Refrigerate until slightly thickened"	Be consistency of unbeaten egg whites	1¼ hours	5 to 6 minutes	Adding creamy ingredients or when mixture will be beaten
"Refrigerate until thickened"	Be thick enough so that a spoon drawn through leaves a definite impression	1½ hours	7 to 8 minutes	Adding solid ingredients such as fruits or vegetables
"Refrigerate until set but not firm"	Stick to finger when touched and should mound or move to the side when bowl or mold is tilted	2 hours	30 minutes	Layering gelatin mixtures
"Refrigerate until firm"	Not stick to finger when touched and not mound or move when mold is tilted	Individual molds: at least 3 hours 2- to 6-cup mold: at least 4 hours 8- to 12-cup mold: at least 5 hours or overnight		Unmolding and serving

Speed set (ice cube) method is not recommended for molding.

Gelatin Consistencies

Gelatin should be consistency of thick syrup.

Set but not firm gelatin should stick to finger when touched and should mound or move to the side when bowl or mold is tilted.

Slightly thickened gelatin should be consistency of unbeaten egg whites.

Firm gelatin should not stick to finger when touched and should not move when mold is tilted.

Thickened gelatin should be thick enough so that a spoon drawn through it leaves a definite inpression.

The Secret to Molding Gelatin

The Mold

• Use metal molds, traditional decorative molds and other metal forms, or plastic molds. You can use square or round cake pans, fluted or plain tube pans, loaf pans, or metal mixing bowls (the nested sets give you a variety of sizes). You can also use metal fruit or juice cans. (To unmold, dip can in warm water, then puncture bottom of can and unmold.)

• To determine the volume of the mold, measure first with water. Most recipes give an indication of the size of the mold needed. For clear gelatin, you need a 2-cup mold for a 4-serving size package and a 4-cup mold for an 8-serving size package.

• If mold holds less than the size called for, pour the extra gelatin into a separate dish. Refrigerate and serve it at another time. Do not use a mold that is too large, since it would be difficult to unmold. Either increase the recipe or use a smaller mold.

• For easier unmolding, spray mold with no stick cooking spray before filling mold.

The Preparation

• To prepare gelatin for molding, use less water than the amount called for on the package. For a 4-serving size package, decrease cold water to ¾ cup. For an 8-serving size package, decrease cold water to 1½ cups. (This adjustment has already been made in the recipes in this publication.) The firmer consistency will result in a less fragile mold. It also makes unmolding much simpler.

• To arrange fruits or vegetables in the mold, refrigerate gelatin until thickened. (If gelatin is not thick enough, fruits or vegetables may sink or float.) Pour gelatin into mold to about ¼-inch depth. Reserve remaining gelatin at room temperature. Arrange fruits or vegetables in decorative pattern on gelatin. Refrigerate mold until gelatin is set but not firm. Spoon reserved gelatin over pattern in mold. Refrigerate until firm, then unmold.

The Unmolding

• First, allow gelatin to set until firm by refrigerating several hours or overnight. Also chill serving plate on which mold is to be served by storing in refrigerator.

• Make certain that gelatin is completely firm. It should not feel sticky on top and should not mound or move to the side if mold is tilted.

• Moisten tips of fingers and gently pull gelatin from around edge of mold. Or, use a small metal spatula or pointed knife dipped in warm water to loosen top edge.

• Dip mold in warm, not hot, water just to rim for about 15 seconds. Lift from water, hold upright and shake to loosen gelatin. Or, gently pull gelatin from edge of mold.

• Moisten chilled serving plate with water. (This allows gelatin to be moved after unmolding.) Place moistened serving plate on top of mold. Invert mold and plate; holding mold and plate together, shake slightly to loosen. Gently remove mold. If gelatin does not release easily, dip mold in warm water again for a few seconds. Center gelatin on serving plate.

Unmolding

1. Before unmolding, gently pull gelatin from around edge of mold with moist fingertips.

4. Place moistened serving plate on top of mold.

2. Dip mold in warm water, just to the rim, for about 15 seconds.

5. Invert mold and plate; shake to loosen gelatin.

3. Lift mold from water, hold upright and shake to loosen gelatin.

6. Remove mold and center gelatin on plate.

Simple Additions

Fruits and Vegetables

• Refrigerate gelatin until thickened. For a 4-serving size package, add ¾ to 1½ cups sliced or chopped fruit or vegetables. (For an 8-serving size package, add 1½ to 3 cups.) Do not use fresh or frozen pineapple, kiwi, gingerroot, papaya, figs or guava. An enzyme in these fruits will prevent the gelatin from setting. However, if cooked or canned, these fruits may be used. Drain canned or fresh fruits well before adding to the gelatin (unless a recipe specifies otherwise). The fruit juice or syrup can be used to replace part of the cold water used in preparing the gelatin.

• Some favorite fresh fruits include apples, bananas, peaches, oranges, grapefruit, melons, grapes, pears, strawberries, blueberries and raspberries. Canned fruits include peaches, pineapple, pears, apricots, mandarin oranges, cherries and fruit cocktail. Dried fruits, such as raisins, currants, figs, dates, apricots or prunes, can be added to gelatin. Nuts, such as coconut, walnuts, pecans and almonds, can also be used.

• Gelatin salads can include fresh vegetables, such as carrots, celery, peppers, onions, cucumbers, tomatoes or summer squash. Serve them on crisp salad greens.

Carbonated Beverages

Substitute cold carbonated beverages, such as seltzer, club soda, fruit-flavored seltzer, ginger ale or a lemon-lime carbonated beverage, for part or all of the cold water. (Do not use tonic water.)

Fruit Juice or Iced Tea

Use fruit juices, such as orange, apple, cranberry, canned pineapple or white grape juice, for part of the cold water. Nectars, such as apricot, peach and mango, or juice blends and drinks can also be substituted. Or, use iced tea, plain or flavored, for part of the cold water.

Citrus Fruits

Adding grated orange, lemon or lime peel and lemon or lime juice will add zing to your gelatin. Add 1 teaspoon grated peel and/or 1 tablespoon juice to a 4-serving size package of gelatin. For an 8-serving size package, use 1½ teaspoons grated peel and 1½ tablespoons juice.

Flavored Extracts

Add just a touch of flavoring extracts, such as vanilla, almond, peppermint or rum, for additional flavor.

PUDDING

The recipes in this publication use both JELL-O Cook & Serve Pudding & Pie Filling, which requires cooking, and JELL-O Instant Pudding & Pie Filling, which is not cooked. These products are not interchangeable in recipes. Be sure to use the product called for in the recipe.

JELL-O Instant Pudding & Pie Filling is also available Fat Free. Both the Instant and the Cook & Serve Pudding & Pie Fillings are also available as Sugar Free Fat Free.

See individual packages for basic directions for preparing the products as either a pudding or a pie filling.

Some Tips for Success

For JELL-O Instant Pudding & Pie Filling

- Always use cold milk. Beat pudding mix slowly, not vigorously.

- For best results, use 2% reduced fat milk or whole milk. Fat-free, 1% lowfat, reconstituted nonfat dry milk or lactose-reduced milk can also be used. For Fat Free or Sugar Free Fat Free Pudding & Pie Filling, use cold fat-free milk.

- Always store prepared pudding desserts, pies and snacks in the refrigerator.

For JELL-O Cook & Serve Pudding & Pie Filling

- It's best to cook the pudding in a heavy saucepan to ensure even heating. Stir pudding mixture constantly as it cooks. Make sure it comes to full boil. The mixture will be thin, but will thicken as it cools.

- For a creamier pudding, place a piece of plastic wrap on the surface of pudding while cooling. Stir before serving.

- To cool pudding quickly, place saucepan of hot pudding in larger pan of ice water; stir frequently until mixture is cooled. Do not use this method for pie filling.

Simple Additions

- Stir mix-ins such as chopped candy bar, chopped cookies, candy-coated milk chocolate candies, peanut butter or butterscotch chips, BAKER'S Semi-Sweet Real Chocolate Chips, miniature marshmallows, nuts or toasted BAKER'S ANGEL FLAKE Coconut into prepared pudding just before serving.

- Stir fruit such as chopped banana or strawberries, raspberries, blueberries, mandarin orange segments or drained canned fruit cocktail into prepared pudding just before serving.

- For spiced pudding, stir ½ teaspoon ground cinnamon into a 4-serving size package of pudding mix before adding cold milk.

NO BAKE CHEESECAKES and DESSERTS

Some Tips for Success

- The cheesecake can also be prepared in an 8- or 9-inch square pan or 12 foil- or paper-lined muffin cups.

- Two packages of the cheesecake can be prepared in a 13×9-inch pan or a 9×3-inch springform pan.

- To serve, dip the pie plate just to the rim in hot water for 30 seconds before cutting.

- To freeze, cover the cheesecake. Freeze up to 2 weeks. Thaw in refrigerator 3 hours before serving.

- For easy cleanup, line the 8- or 9-inch square pan with foil before preparing the No Bake Dessert.

- The No Bake Desserts can also be served frozen. Freeze 4 hours or until firm. Remove from freezer and serve immediately.

Shimmering Molds

Cranberry Fruit Mold

Experience delicious fruit-filled effervescence in this delightful mold!

> 2 cups boiling water
> 1 package (8-serving size) or 2 packages (4-serving size) JELL-O®
>   Brand Cranberry Flavor Gelatin Dessert or JELL-O® Brand
>   Cranberry Flavor Sugar Free Low Calorie Gelatin Dessert
> 1½ cups cold juice, ginger ale, lemon-lime carbonated beverage,
>   seltzer or water
> 2 cups halved green and/or red seedless grapes
> 1 can (11 ounces) mandarin orange segments, drained

STIR boiling water into gelatin in large bowl at least 2 minutes until completely dissolved. Stir in cold juice. Refrigerate about 1½ hours or until thickened (spoon drawn through leaves definite impression). Stir in fruit. Spoon into 6-cup mold.

REFRIGERATE 4 hours or until firm. Unmold. Garnish as desired.

Makes 10 servings

Preparation Time: 15 minutes
Refrigerating Time: 5½ hours

Cranberry Fruit Mold

Mimosa Mold

1½ cups boiling water
1 package (8-serving size) or 2 packages (4-serving size) JELL-O®
    Brand Sparkling White Grape or Lemon Flavor Gelatin Dessert
2 cups cold seltzer or club soda
1 can (11 ounces) mandarin orange segments, drained
1 cup sliced strawberries

STIR boiling water into gelatin in large bowl at least 2 minutes or until completely dissolved. Refrigerate 15 minutes. Gently stir in seltzer. Refrigerate about 30 minutes or until slightly thickened (consistency of unbeaten egg whites.) Gently stir about 15 seconds. Stir in oranges and strawberries. Pour into 6-cup mold.

REFRIGERATE 4 hours or until firm. Unmold. Garnish as desired. Store leftover gelatin mold in refrigerator. *Makes 12 servings*

Preparation Time: 15 minutes
Refrigerating Time: 4¾ hours

Gelatin molds can be as simple or elaborate as you wish to make them, but they are always impressive. A great garnish for this mold is a heaping spoonful of COOL WHIP Whipped Topping and additional fresh fruit.

Mimosa Mold

Melon Salad

A wonderful summer refresher.

  2½ cups boiling apple juice
  1 package (8-serving size) or 2 packages (4-serving size) JELL-O®
      Brand Watermelon Flavor Sugar Free Low Calorie Gelatin
      Dessert or JELL-O® Brand Watermelon Flavor Gelatin Dessert
  1½ cups cold seltzer or club soda
  1 teaspoon lemon juice
  2 cups cantaloupe and honeydew melon cubes

STIR boiling juice into gelatin in large bowl at least 2 minutes until completely dissolved. Stir in cold seltzer and lemon juice. Refrigerate about 1½ hours or until thickened (spoon drawn through leaves definite impression). Stir in melon cubes. Spoon into 6-cup mold.

REFRIGERATE 4 hours or until firm. Unmold. Garnish as desired.

Makes 10 servings

Preparation Time: 15 minutes
Refrigerating Time: 5½ hours

This flavorful watermelon gelatin was introduced in 1990 to appeal to kids but has become a hit with adults as well. It's especially refreshing with fresh summer fruits. Any red flavor gelatin may be substituted for the watermelon, if desired.

Melon Salad

Sparkling Berry Salad

This berry-filled mold captures the freshness of spring.

> 2 cups boiling diet cranberry juice cocktail
> 1 package (8-serving size) or 2 packages (4-serving size) JELL-O®
>   Brand Sugar Free Low Calorie Gelatin Dessert or JELL-O®
>   Brand Gelatin Dessert, any red flavor
> 1½ cups cold seltzer or club soda
> ¼ cup creme de cassis liqueur (optional)
> 1 teaspoon lemon juice
> 3 cups assorted berries (blueberries, raspberries and sliced
>   strawberries), divided

STIR boiling cranberry juice into gelatin in large bowl at least 2 minutes until completely dissolved. Stir in cold seltzer, liqueur and lemon juice. Refrigerate about 1½ hours or until slightly thickened (consistency of unbeaten egg whites).

STIR in 2 cups of the berries. Spoon into 5-cup mold.

REFRIGERATE 4 hours or until firm. Unmold. Top with remaining 1 cup berries. *Makes 8 servings*

Preparation Time: 15 minutes
Refrigerating Time: 5½ hours

Fruit should be added to gelatin that has been chilled until it thickens, but is not yet set. This way the fruit will remain suspended in the gelatin.

Sparkling Berry Salad

Layered Orange Pineapple Mold

This creamy mold with a jewel-like crown goes beautifully with baked ham.

> 1 can (20 ounces) crushed pineapple in juice, undrained
> Cold water
> 1½ cups boiling water
> 1 package (8-serving size) or 2 packages (4-serving size) JELL-O®
> Brand Orange Flavor Gelatin Dessert
> 1 package (8 ounces) PHILADELPHIA® Cream Cheese, softened

DRAIN pineapple, reserving juice. Add cold water to juice to make 1½ cups.

STIR boiling water into gelatin in large bowl at least 2 minutes until completely dissolved. Stir in measured pineapple juice and water. Reserve 1 cup gelatin at room temperature.

STIR ½ of the crushed pineapple into remaining gelatin. Pour into 6-cup mold. Refrigerate about 2 hours or until set but not firm (gelatin should stick to finger when touched and should mound).

STIR reserved 1 cup gelatin gradually into cream cheese in medium bowl with wire whisk until smooth. Stir in remaining crushed pineapple. Pour over gelatin layer in mold.

REFRIGERATE 4 hours or until firm. Unmold. Garnish as desired.

Makes 10 servings

Preparation Time: 20 minutes
Refrigerating Time: 6 hours

Layered Orange Pineapple Mold

Snack Attacks

Juicy JELL-O®

1 cup boiling water
1 package (4-serving size) JELL-O® Brand Gelatin, any flavor
1 cup cold juice, any flavor

STIR boiling water into gelatin in medium bowl at least 2 minutes until completely dissolved. Stir in cold juice.

REFRIGERATE 4 hours or until firm.   *Makes 4 (¹/₂-cup) servings*

Note: *Do not use fresh or frozen pineapple, kiwi, papaya or guava juice. Gelatin will not set.*

Variation: *For fruited Juicy JELL-O®, prepare as directed but refrigerate for just 30 minutes until slightly thickened. Stir in 1 cup raspberries, blueberries or chopped strawberries. Refrigerate 4 hours or until firm.*

Preparation Time: 5 minutes plus refrigerating

Juicy JELL-O®

5-Minute Chocolate Banana Parfait

   2 cups cold fat free milk
   1 package (4-serving size) JELL-O® Chocolate Flavor Fat Free
      Sugar Free Instant Reduced Calorie Pudding
   2 medium bananas, sliced
   ½ cup thawed COOL WHIP LITE® Whipped Topping
   1 tablespoon chopped walnuts, optional

POUR milk into medium bowl. Add pudding mix. Beat with wire whisk 2 minutes.

SPOON ½ of pudding evenly into 4 dessert glasses. Layer with banana slices, whipped topping and remaining pudding.

GARNISH each serving with additional banana slices, whipped topping and walnuts, if desired. *Makes 4 servings*

Preparation Time: 5 minutes

Aquarium Cups

   ¾ cup boiling water
   1 package (4-serving size) JELL-O® Brand Berry Blue Flavor
      Gelatin Dessert
   ½ cup cold water
      Ice cubes
      Gummy fish

STIR boiling water into gelatin in medium bowl at least 2 minutes until completely dissolved. Mix cold water and ice cubes to make 1¼ cups. Add to gelatin, stirring until slightly thickened. Remove any remaining ice. (If mixture is still thin, refrigerate until slightly thickened.)

POUR thickened gelatin into 4 dessert dishes. Suspend gummy fish in gelatin. Refrigerate 1 hour or until firm. *Makes 4 servings*

Preparation Time: 10 minutes
Refrigerating Time: 1 hour

5-Minute Chocolate Banana Parfaits

Pudding Café

The addition of flavored coffees to this creamy snack makes it a favorite with adults.

> **2 cups cold milk**
> **1 package (4-serving size) JELL-O® Chocolate or Vanilla Flavor Instant Pudding & Pie Filling**
> **¼ cup GENERAL FOODS INTERNATIONAL COFFEES®, any flavor**

POUR milk into medium bowl. Add pudding mix and flavored instant coffee. Beat with wire whisk 2 minutes. Refrigerate 2 hours or until ready to serve.

Makes 4 servings

Preparation Time: 5 minutes
Refrigerating Time: 2 hours

Cinnamon Chocolate Pudding

> **2 cups cold milk**
> **1 package (4-serving size) JELL-O® Chocolate Flavor Instant Pudding & Pie Filling**
> **½ teaspoon ground cinnamon**
> **½ cup thawed COOL WHIP® Whipped Topping**

POUR milk into medium bowl. Add pudding mix and cinnamon. Beat with wire whisk 1 minute. Gently stir in whipped topping. Spoon into dessert dishes.

REFRIGERATE until ready to serve.

Makes 5 servings

Preparation Time: 5 minutes
Refrigerating Time: 2 hours

Juicy Parfaits

2 cups boiling water, divided
1 package (4-serving size) JELL-O® Brand Raspberry Flavor Gelatin
    Dessert or any red flavor
1 package (4-serving size) JELL-O® Brand Lemon Flavor Gelatin
    Dessert or any non-red flavor
2 cups cold juice, any flavor, divided
1 tub (8 ounces) COOL WHIP® Whipped Topping, thawed

STIR 1 cup of the boiling water into each flavor gelatin in separate bowls at least 2 minutes until completely dissolved. Stir 1 cup cold juice into each bowl. Pour into separate 9×9-inch pans.

REFRIGERATE 4 hours or until firm. Cut each pan into ½-inch cubes. Layer alternating flavors and whipped topping into 8 dessert glasses. Garnish with additional whipped topping, if desired.

Makes 8 servings

Note: *Do not use fresh or frozen pineapple, kiwi, papaya or guava juice. Gelatin will not set.*

Preparation Time: 10 minutes
Refrigerating Time: 4 hours

Juice Up Your JELL-O

Fruity Gelatin Pops

These super after-school treats couldn't be easier!

> **1 cup boiling water**
> **1 package (4-serving size) JELL-O® Brand Gelatin Dessert, any flavor**
> **⅓ cup sugar**
> **1⅓ cups cold juice, any flavor**
> **6 (5-ounce) paper cups**

STIR boiling water into gelatin and sugar in medium bowl at least 2 minutes until completely dissolved. Stir in cold juice. Pour into cups. Freeze about 2 hours or until almost firm. Insert wooden pop stick into each for handle.

FREEZE 5 hours or overnight until firm. To remove pop from cup, place bottom of cup under warm running water for 15 seconds. Press firmly on bottom of cup to release pop. (Do not twist or pull pop stick.) Store leftover pops in freezer up to 2 weeks.   *Makes 6 pops*

Outrageous Orange Pops: *Use 1 cup boiling water, JELL-O® Brand Orange Flavor Gelatin Dessert, ⅓ cup sugar and 1⅓ cups orange juice.*

Fruity Strawberry Pops: *Use 1 cup boiling water, JELL-O® Brand Strawberry Flavor Gelatin Dessert, ⅓ cup sugar, ⅔ cup cold water and ⅔ cup puréed strawberries.*

Fizzy Grape Pops: *Use 1 cup boiling water, JELL-O® Brand Sparkling White Grape Flavor Gelatin Dessert, 2 tablespoons sugar and 1½ cups carbonated grape beverage.*

Lemonade Pops: *Use 1 cup boiling water, JELL-O® Brand Lemon Flavor Gelatin Dessert, ⅓ cup sugar, 1 cup cold water and 2 tablespoons lemon juice.*

Iced Tea Pops: *Use 1 cup boiling water, JELL-O® Brand Lemon Flavor Gelatin Dessert, 2 tablespoons sugar and 1½ cups pre-sweetened iced tea.*

Preparation Time: 10 minutes
Freezing Time: 7 hours

Juice Up Your JELL-O

Fruity Gelatin Pops

Easy Pudding Milk Shake

In just minutes, you can whip up this creamy milk shake—enough for the entire family.

> **3 cups cold milk**
> **1 package (4-serving size) JELL-O® Instant Pudding & Pie Filling, any flavor**
> **1½ cups ice cream, any flavor**

POUR milk into blender container. Add pudding mix and ice cream; cover. Blend on high speed 30 seconds or until smooth. Pour into glasses and garnish as desired. Serve immediately.   *Makes 5 servings*

Preparation Time: 5 minutes

Jell-O Jigglers® Snack Pops

Jigglers® on sticks—like lollipops!

> **1¼ cups boiling water**
> **1 package (8-serving size) or 2 packages (4-serving size) JELL-O® Brand Gelatin Dessert, any flavor**
> **4 (5-ounce) paper cups**
> **6 plastic straws, cut in half**

STIR boiling water into gelatin in medium bowl at least 3 minutes until completely dissolved. Cool 15 minutes at room temperature. Pour into cups.

REFRIGERATE 3 hours or until firm. Carefully peel away cups. Using a knife dipped in warm water, cut each gelatin cup horizontally into 3 round slices. Insert straw into each gelatin slice to resemble a lollipop.

Makes 12 pops

Preparation Time: 10 minutes
Refrigerating Time: 3 hours

Easy Pudding Milk Shakes

Juicy Berry Sorbet

¾ cup boiling water
1 package (4-serving size) JELL-O® Brand Raspberry or Strawberry
     Flavor Gelatin
½ cup sugar
2 cups cold juice, any flavor

STIR boiling water into gelatin and sugar in large bowl at least 2 minutes until completely dissolved. Stir in cold juice. Pour into 9-inch square pan.

FREEZE about 1 hour or until ice crystals form 1 inch around edges. Spoon into blender container; cover. Blend on high speed about 30 seconds or until smooth. Return to pan. Freeze 6 hours or overnight until firm. Scoop into dessert dishes. Store leftover sorbet in freezer.

Preparation Time: 10 minutes
Freezing Time: 7 hours

Strawberry Banana Smoothie

Satisfy the between-meal "hungries" with this yummy drink.

2 cups crushed ice
1 cup cold milk
1 package (4-serving size) JELL-O® Brand Strawberry Flavor
     Gelatin Dessert
1 container (8 ounces) BREYERS® Vanilla Lowfat Yogurt
1 large banana, cut into chunks

PLACE all ingredients in blender container; cover. Blend on high speed 30 seconds or until smooth. Serve immediately.   *Makes 4 servings*

Preparation Time: 5 minutes

Juicy Berry Sorbet

SNACK ATTACKS

Frozen Pudding Cookiewiches®

Keep these treats on hand in the freezer for last-minute snacks.

 1½ **cups cold milk**
  ½ **cup peanut butter**
  1 **package (4-serving size) JELL-O® Instant Pudding & Pie Filling,
     any flavor**
 24 **graham crackers**
    Colored sprinkles

STIR milk gradually into peanut butter in deep narrow bottomed bowl until smooth. Add pudding mix. Beat with wire whisk 2 minutes. Let stand 5 minutes.

SPREAD pudding mixture about ½-inch thick onto 12 of the crackers. Top with remaining crackers, pressing lightly and smoothing around edges with spatula. Coat edges with sprinkles.

FREEZE 3 hours or until firm.   *Makes 12*

Preparation Time: 15 minutes
Freezing Time: 3 hours

Pudding Mix-Ins

  2 **cups cold milk**
  1 **package (4-serving size) JELL-O® Instant Pudding & Pie Filling,
     any flavor**
    **Assorted "treasures": BAKER'S® Semi-Sweet Real Chocolate
     Chips, chopped nuts, miniature marshmallows, raisins,
     chopped bananas, halved grapes, crumbled chocolate sandwich
     cookies or peanut butter**
  Thawed COOL WHIP® Whipped Topping

POUR milk into medium bowl. Add pudding mix. Beat with wire whisk 2 minutes.

PLACE 1 tablespoon of the "treasures" into each of 4 dessert glasses. Spoon pudding over treasures.

REFRIGERATE until ready to serve. Top with whipped topping and garnish as desired.   *Makes 4 servings*

Preparation Time: 5 minutes
Refrigerating Time: 2 hours

Florida Sunshine Cups

¾ cup boiling water
1 package (4-serving size) JELL-O® Brand Sugar Free Low Calorie Orange or Lemon Flavor Gelatin
1 cup cold orange juice, any variety
½ cup fresh raspberries
½ cup fresh orange sections, halved

STIR boiling water into gelatin in large bowl at least 2 minutes until completely dissolved. Stir in cold juice. Refrigerate 1½ hours or until thickened (spoon drawn through leaves definite impression).

MEASURE ¾ cup thickened gelatin into medium bowl; set aside. Stir fruit into remaining gelatin. Pour into serving bowl or 6 dessert dishes.

BEAT reserved gelatin with electric mixer on high speed until fluffy and about doubled in volume. Spoon over gelatin in bowl or dishes.

REFRIGERATE 3 hours or until firm. Store leftover gelatin in refrigerator. *Makes 6 servings*

Preparation Time: 20 minutes
Refrigerating Time: 4½ hours

5-Minute Mousse

1½ cups cold milk
1 package (4-serving size) JELL-O® Instant Pudding & Pie Filling,
  any flavor
1½ cups thawed COOL WHIP® Whipped Topping, divided

POUR milk into large bowl. Add pudding mix. Beat with wire whisk
2 minutes.

STIR in 1 cup whipped topping. Spoon into individual dessert dishes or
serving bowl.

REFRIGERATE until ready to serve. Top with remaining whipped
topping and garnish as desired.   *Makes 5 servings*

*Variation: Prepare recipe as directed above using fat free milk, any
flavor JELL-O® Fat Free Sugar Free Instant Reduced Calorie Pudding &
Pie Filling and COOL WHIP FREE® or COOL WHIP LITE® Whipped
Topping.*

Preparation Time: 5 minutes
Refrigerating Time: 2 hours

JELL-O® Fun Facts

*For an extra decadent treat, drizzle this
no-fuss mousse with your favorite chocolate
fudge or caramel sauce and garnish with a
rich store-bought chocolate-covered cookie.
Your guests will be impressed!*

5-Minute Mousse

Chocolate Peanut Butter Parfaits

Yummm! Luscious layers of two favorite flavors.

 3 tablespoons milk
 3 tablespoons peanut butter
 1 cup thawed COOL WHIP® Whipped Topping
 2 cups cold milk
 1 package (4-serving size) JELL-O® Chocolate Flavor Instant
     Pudding & Pie Filling
 ¼ cup chopped peanuts

STIR 3 tablespoons milk into peanut butter in medium bowl until smooth. Gently stir in whipped topping.

POUR 2 cups milk into medium bowl. Add pudding mix. Beat with wire whisk 2 minutes. Alternately spoon whipped topping mixture and pudding into 6 parfait glasses.

REFRIGERATE until ready to serve. Sprinkle with peanuts.

Makes 6 servings

Preparation Time: 5 minutes

For a fast, fabulous and refreshing version of this recipe, substitute JELL-O Lemon Flavor Instant Pudding for the chocolate pudding and prepare as above, omitting the peanut butter and 3 tablespoons milk from the Cool Whip mixture. Sprinkle with your favorite fresh fruit instead of peanuts!

Chocolate Peanut Butter Parfaits

Frozen Creamy Pudding Pops

1½ cups cold milk
  1 package (4-serving size) JELL-O® Instant Pudding & Pie Filling,
    any flavor
  2 cups thawed COOL WHIP® Whipped Topping
  9 (5-ounce) paper or plastic cups or popsicle molds

ADDITIONS
  ½ cup chopped cookies
  ½ cup chopped toffee candy
  ½ cup mashed banana
  ½ cup miniature marshmallows and ¼ cup each chopped peanuts
    and BAKER'S Semi-Sweet Real Chocolate Chips

POUR milk into medium bowl. Add pudding mix. Beat with wire whisk
2 minutes. Gently stir in whipped topping. Stir in desired Special
Additions. Spoon into cups. Insert wooden pop stick into each for
handle.

FREEZE 5 hours or overnight. To remove pop from cup, place bottom
of cup under running water for 15 seconds. Press firmly on bottom of
cup to release pop. (Do not twist or pull pop stick.)   *Makes 9 pops*

Special Additions: *Stir in ¼ cup GENERAL FOODS INTERNATIONAL*
COFFEES®, any flavor, with pudding mix.

Preparation Time: 10 minutes

For a quick twist on this recipe, make
pops in ice cube trays in different flavors
and place in a large glass bowl for a fun
"kids" table centerpiece. For a variation,
add fresh blueberries or chopped
strawberries to pops or cubes.

Pudding in a Cloud

How to please the family in just 15 minutes. Amuse the kids by letting them make faces on the pudding with pieces of marshmallow, gumdrops or decorating gel.

> **2 cups thawed COOL WHIP® Whipped Topping**
> **2 cups cold milk**
> **1 package (4-serving size) JELL-O® Instant Pudding & Pie Filling, any flavor**

SPOON whipped topping evenly into 6 dessert dishes. Using back of spoon, spread whipped topping onto bottom and up side of each dish.

POUR milk into medium bowl. Add pudding mix. Beat with wire whisk 2 minutes. Let stand 5 minutes. Spoon pudding into center of whipped topping.

REFRIGERATE until ready to serve.   *Makes 6 servings*

Preparation Time: 15 minutes
Refrigerating Time: 2 hours

JELL-O® Juicy Jigglers®

> **2½ cups boiling juice (Do not add cold water)**
> **2 packages (8-serving size) or 4 packages (4-serving size) JELL-O® Brand Gelatin Dessert, any flavor**

STIR boiling juice into gelatin in large bowl at least 3 minutes until completely dissolved. Pour into 13×9-inch pan.

REFRIGERATE 3 hours or until firm (does not stick to finger when touched). Dip bottom of pan in warm water about 15 seconds. Cut into decorative shapes with cookie cutters all the way through gelatin or cut into 1-inch squares. Lift from pan.   *Makes about 24 pieces*

Note: *Recipe can be halved. Use 8- or 9-inch square pan.*

Preparation Time: 10 minutes
Refrigerating Time: 3 hours

All-Time Favorites

Miniature Cheesecakes

Add a candle to each of these desserts for a quick birthday party treat.

> 1 package (11.1 ounces) JELL-O® No Bake Real Cheesecake
> 2 tablespoons sugar
> ⅓ cup butter or margarine, melted
> 1½ cups cold milk
> 2 squares BAKER'S® Semi-Sweet Baking Chocolate, melted (optional)

MIX crumbs from mix, sugar and butter thoroughly with fork in medium bowl until crumbs are well moistened. Press onto bottoms of 12 paper-lined or foil-lined muffin cups.

BEAT milk and filling mix with electric mixer on low speed until blended. Beat on medium speed 3 minutes. (Filling will be thick.) Spoon over crumb mixture in muffin cups. Drizzle with melted chocolate, if desired.

REFRIGERATE at least 1 hour or until ready to serve. Garnish as desired. *Makes 12 servings*

Preparation Time: 15 minutes
Refrigerating Time: 1 hour

Miniature Cheesecakes

Watergate Salad
(Pistachio Pineapple Delight)

1 package (4-serving size) JELL-O® Pistachio Flavor Instant
    Pudding & Pie Filling
1 can (20 ounces) crushed pineapple in juice, undrained
1 cup miniature marshmallows
½ cup chopped nuts
2 cups thawed COOL WHIP® Whipped Topping

STIR pudding mix, pineapple with juice, marshmallows and nuts in large bowl until well blended. Gently stir in whipped topping.

REFRIGERATE 1 hour or until ready to serve. Garnish as desired.

Makes 8 servings

Preparation Time: 10 minutes
Refrigerating Time: 1 hour

JELL-O® Fun Facts

Originally named Pistachio Pineapple Delight, this salad first surfaced in 1976, the year Pistachio Flavor Instant Pudding & Pie Filling was launched. This recipe doubles as an accompaniment for your favorite poultry dish or simply as a dessert and continues to be one of our most requested recipes.

Watergate Salad (Pistachio Pineapple Delight)

Southern Banana Pudding

A classic expression of Southern hospitality.

    1 package (4-serving size) JELL-O® Vanilla or Banana Cream Flavor Cook & Serve Pudding & Pie Filling *(not Instant)*
2½ cups milk
2 egg yolks, well beaten
30 to 35 vanilla wafers
2 large bananas, sliced
2 egg whites
Dash salt
¼ cup sugar

HEAT oven to 350°F.

STIR pudding mix into milk in medium saucepan. Add egg yolks. Stirring constantly, cook on medium heat until mixture comes to full boil. Remove from heat.

ARRANGE layer of cookies on bottom and up side of 1½-quart baking dish. Add layer of banana slices; top with ⅓ of the pudding. Repeat layers twice, ending with pudding.

BEAT egg whites and salt in medium bowl with electric mixer on high speed until foamy. Gradually add sugar, beating until stiff peaks form. Spoon meringue mixture lightly onto pudding, spreading to edge of dish to seal.

BAKE 10 to 15 minutes or until meringue is lightly browned. Serve warm or refrigerate until ready to serve.   *Makes 8 servings*

Preparation Time: 30 minutes
Baking Time: 15 minutes

Southern Banana Pudding

Chocolate Cherry Cheesecake

**2 packages (21.4 ounces each) JELL-O® No Bake Cherry or
Strawberry Topped Cheesecake**
¼ cup sugar
¾ cup butter or margarine, melted
2½ cups cold milk
**3 squares BAKER'S® Semi-Sweet Baking Chocolate, melted and
cooled**

STIR crust mixes, sugar, butter and 2 tablespoons water with fork in medium bowl until crumbs are well moistened. First, firmly press ½ of crumbs 2 inches up side of 9-inch springform pan. Press remaining crumbs firmly onto bottom, using measuring cup. Spoon 1 fruit pouch over crust.

POUR cold milk into medium mixing bowl. Add Filling Mixes. Beat with electric mixer on lowest speed until blended. Beat on medium speed 3 minutes. Filling will be thick. Immediately stir 1 cup cheesecake mixture into chocolate until blended. Spoon mixture over fruit in crust. Top with remaining fruit pouch.

REFRIGERATE 4 hours or until firm. To serve, run a small knife or spatula around side of pan to loosen crust; remove side of pan.

Makes 16 servings

Note: *Cheesecake can also be prepared in a 13×9-inch baking pan, pressing all of the crust firmly onto bottom of pan. Continue as directed.*

Preparation Time: 15 minutes plus refrigerating

Gelatin Poke Cake

This fun cake can be made with any one of the JELL-O® gelatin flavors.

- **1 package (2-layer size) white cake mix or cake mix with pudding in the mix**
- **1 cup boiling water**
- **1 package (4-serving size) JELL-O® Brand Gelatin Dessert, any flavor**
- **½ cup cold water**
- **1 tub (8 ounces) COOL WHIP® Whipped Topping, thawed**

HEAT oven to 350°F.

PREPARE and bake cake mix as directed on package for 13×9-inch baking pan. Remove from oven. Cool cake in pan 15 minutes. Pierce cake with large fork at ½-inch intervals.

MEANWHILE, stir boiling water into gelatin in medium bowl at least 2 minutes until completely dissolved. Stir in cold water; carefully pour over cake. Refrigerate 3 hours.

FROST with whipped topping. Refrigerate at least 1 hour or until ready to serve. Decorate as desired.   *Makes 15 servings*

Preparation Time: 15 minutes
Baking Time: 35 minutes
Refrigerating Time: 4 hours

JELL-O® Fun Facts

This classic recipe can be made as cup cakes or a layer cake. Also, by simply changing the flavor of gelatin, you can tailor it to suit your favorite holiday. For example, red for Valentine's Day or orange for Halloween.

Creamy Vanilla Sauce

3½ cups cold milk, light cream or half-and-half
1 package (4-serving size) JELL-O® Vanilla or French Vanilla Flavor
  Instant Pudding & Pie Filling

POUR milk into bowl. Add pudding mix. Beat with wire whisk
2 minutes. Cover.

REFRIGERATE until ready to serve. Serve over your favorite fruits or
cake. Garnish as desired.   *Makes 3½ cups*

Creamy Citrus Sauce: *Add 2 teaspoons grated orange peel with pudding
mix.*

Preparation Time: 5 minutes

Frozen Cheesecake Pie

1 package (21.4 ounces) JELL-O® No Bake Cherry or Strawberry
  Topped Cheesecake
2 tablespoons sugar
⅓ cup butter or margarine, melted
1½ cups cold milk
1 tub (8 ounces) COOL WHIP® Whipped Topping, thawed

MIX crumbs, sugar and butter thoroughly with fork in 9-inch pie plate
until crumbs are well moistened. Press firmly against side of plate first,
using finger or large spoon to shape edge. Press remaining crumbs
firmly onto bottom using measuring cup.

BEAT milk and filling mix in medium bowl with electric mixer on low
speed until blended. Beat on medium speed 3 minutes. (Filling will be
thick.) Stir in whipped topping until smooth. Swirl fruit topping into
mixture with spatula. Spoon into crust.

FREEZE 6 hours or overnight until firm. Let stand at room
temperature or in refrigerator 15 minutes or until pie can be cut easily.
                                                        Makes 8 servings

Preparation Time: 15 minutes
Freezing Time: 6 hours

Creamy Vanilla Sauce

Luscious Pies

Cookies & Creme Café Pie

> 1 package (12.6 ounces) JELL-O® No Bake Cookies & Creme Dessert
> ⅓ cup butter or margarine, melted
> 1⅓ cups cold milk
> ¼ cup **GENERAL FOODS INTERNATIONAL COFFEE**®, Suisse Mocha Flavor, Vanilla Café Flavor or Irish Cream Café Flavor

STIR crust mix and butter thoroughly with spoon in medium bowl until crumbs are well moistened. Press onto bottom and up side of 9-inch pie plate.

POUR cold milk into large bowl. Add filling mix and coffee. Beat with electric mixer on low speed 30 seconds. Beat on high speed 3 minutes. **Do not underbeat.**

RESERVE ½ cup of the crushed cookies. Gently stir remaining crushed cookies into filling until well blended. Spoon mixture into prepared pie crust. Top with reserved cookies. Refrigerate 4 hours or until firm or freeze 2 hours to serve frozen. *Makes 8 servings*

Preparation Time: 15 minutes plus refrigerating

Cookies & Creme Café Pie

No Bake Cappuccino Cheesecake

The flavors of coffee and cinnamon add spark to this sophisticated dessert.

> 1 package (11.1 ounces) JELL-O® No Bake Real Cheesecake
> 2 tablespoons sugar
> ⅓ cup butter or margarine, melted
> 2 teaspoons MAXWELL HOUSE® Instant Coffee
> 1½ cups cold milk
> ¼ teaspoon ground cinnamon

MIX crumbs, sugar and butter thoroughly with fork in 9-inch pie plate until crumbs are well moistened. Press firmly against side of pie plate first, using finger or large spoon to shape edge. Press remaining crumbs firmly onto bottom using measuring cup.

DISSOLVE coffee in milk. Beat milk mixture, filling mix and cinnamon with electric mixer on low speed until blended. Beat on medium speed 3 minutes. (Filling will be thick.) Spoon into crust. Garnish with crushed chocolate sandwich cookies, if desired.

REFRIGERATE at least 1 hour.   *Makes 8 servings*

Preparation Time: 15 minutes
Refrigerating Time: 1 hour

JELL-O® Fun Facts

If you are having a crowd, this is a perfect recipe to make. Just double all the ingredients and use a 13×9-inch pan. For an extra special garnish, serve each square with a spoonful of COOL WHIP Whipped topping and a chocolate covered coffee bean.

No Bake Cappuccino Cheesecake

COOL 'N EASY® Pie

Ten minutes in the morning—luscious strawberry pie in the evening!

⅔ **cup boiling water**
1 **package (4-serving size) JELL-O® Brand Gelatin, any flavor**
½ **cup cold juice, any flavor**
 Ice cubes
1 **tub (8 ounces) COOL WHIP® Whipped Topping, thawed**
1 **prepared graham cracker crumb crust (6 ounces)**
 Assorted fruit (optional)

STIR boiling water into gelatin in large bowl 2 minutes or until completely dissolved. Mix cold juice and ice to make 1 cup. Add to gelatin, stirring until slightly thickened. Remove any remaining ice.

STIR in whipped topping with wire whisk until smooth. Refrigerate 10 to 15 minutes or until mixture is very thick and will mound. Spoon into crust.

REFRIGERATE 4 hours or until firm. Just before serving, garnish with fruit and additional whipped topping, if desired. Store leftover pie in refrigerator. *Makes 8 servings*

JELL-O® Fun Facts

This refreshing pie, which is a mixture of gelatin and whipped topping, can be easily transformed into any flavor by using different combinations of JELL-O gelatin, fruit and juice.

COOL 'N EASY® Pie

Juicy Triple Berry Pie

   3 cups assorted berries
   1 graham cracker crumb or shortbread pie crust (6 ounces)
   ½ cup sugar
   2 tablespoons cornstarch
 1½ cups orange or orange strawberry banana juice
   1 package (4-serving size) JELL-O® Brand Gelatin, any red flavor

ARRANGE berries in crust.

MIX sugar and cornstarch in medium saucepan. Gradually stir in juice until smooth. Stirring constantly, cook over medium heat until mixture comes to a boil; boil 1 minute. Remove from heat. Stir in gelatin until completely dissolved. Cool to room temperature; pour into crust.

REFRIGERATE 3 hours or until firm. Garnish with COOL WHIP® Whipped Topping, if desired. Store leftover pie in refrigerator.

Makes 8 servings

Preparation Time: 20 minutes
Refrigerating Time: 3 hours

JELL-O® Fun Facts

For an interesting flavor combination, use JELL-O Lemon Flavor Gelatin in place of red gelatin and 1½ cups fresh blueberries in place of strawberries.

5-Minute Double Layer Pie

1¼ cups cold milk
  2 packages (4-serving size each) JELL-O® Instant Pudding & Pie
    Filling, Chocolate Flavor, Lemon Flavor or other flavor
  1 tub (8 ounces) COOL WHIP® Whipped Topping, thawed, divided
  1 prepared graham cracker crumb crust or chocolate pie crust
    (6 ounces or 9 inches)

BEAT milk, pudding mixes and ½ of the whipped topping in medium bowl with wire whisk 1 minute (mixture will be thick). Spread in crust.

SPREAD remaining whipped topping over pudding layer in crust. Refrigerate until ready to serve.   *Makes 8 servings*

Preparation Time: 5 minutes

Ice Cream Pudding Pie

  1 cup cold milk
  1 cup ice cream (any flavor), softened
  1 package (4-serving size) JELL-O® Instant Pudding & Pie Filling,
    any flavor
  1 prepared graham cracker crumb crust (6 ounces)

MIX milk and ice cream in large bowl. Add pudding mix. Beat with electric mixer on lowest speed 1 minute. Pour immediately into crust.

REFRIGERATE 2 hours or until set.   *Makes 8 servings*

Preparation Time: 10 minutes
Refrigerating Time: 2 hours

Frozen Banana Split Pie

The family will go nuts over this ice cream parlor dessert!

  1½ **bananas, sliced**
    1 **prepared graham cracker crumb crust (6 ounces)**
    2 **cups cold milk**
    1 **package (4-serving size) JELL-O® Vanilla or Banana Cream Flavor**
        Instant Pudding & Pie Filling
    1 **tub (8 ounces) COOL WHIP® Whipped Topping, thawed**
        Chocolate, strawberry and pineapple dessert toppings
        Additional banana slices
        Chopped nuts

ARRANGE banana slices on bottom of crust; set aside.

POUR milk into large bowl. Add pudding mix. Beat with wire whisk 1 minute. Gently stir in 2 cups of the whipped topping. Spread over banana slices.

FREEZE 6 hours or until firm. Let stand at room temperature or in refrigerator 15 minutes or until pie can be cut easily. Top with dessert toppings, remaining whipped topping, banana slices and nuts.

Makes 8 servings

Preparation Time: 15 minutes
Freezing Time: 6 hours

JELL-O® Fun Facts

A great way to have fun with this pie is to slice up the pie and serve buffet style. Set out all different kinds of ice cream candy toppings and let everyone individualize their own slice.

Frozen Banana Split Pie

Key Lime Pie

Taste this cool summertime treat.

1¾ cups boiling water
1 package (8-serving size) or 2 packages (4-serving size) JELL-O®
    Brand Lime Flavor Gelatin Dessert
2 teaspoons grated lime peel
¼ cup lime juice
1 pint (2 cups) vanilla ice cream, softened
1 prepared graham cracker crumb crust (6 ounces)

STIR boiling water into gelatin in large bowl at least 2 minutes until completely dissolved. Stir in lime peel and juice.

STIR in ice cream until melted and smooth. Refrigerate 15 to 20 minutes or until mixture is very thick and will mound. Spoon into crust.

REFRIGERATE 2 hours or until firm. Garnish as desired.

Makes 8 servings

Preparation Time: 15 minutes
Refrigerating Time: 2½ hours

Key lime pie is typically made with small tart limes grown in Florida, not generally available in the rest of the U.S. This recipe is a quick and easy adaptation.

Key Lime Pie

Sensational Desserts

Peanut Butter Loaf

1 package (16.1 ounces) JELL-O® No Bake Peanut Butter Cup Dessert
⅓ cup butter or margarine, melted
1⅓ cups cold milk

PLACE topping pouch in large bowl of boiling water; set aside. Line 9×5-inch loaf pan with foil. Stir crust mix and butter with fork in medium bowl until crumbs are well moistened. Press ½ of crumbs firmly onto bottom of prepared pan; reserve remaining crumbs.

POUR cold milk into medium mixing bowl. Add filling mix and peanut butter. Beat with electric mixer on lowest speed until blended. Beat on high speed 3 minutes. **Do not underbeat.** Spoon ½ of filling mixture over crust in pan.

REMOVE pouch from water. Shake vigorously 60 seconds until topping is no longer lumpy. Squeeze ½ of topping over filling in pan. Repeat layers with remaining crumbs and filling. Freeze 4 hours or overnight. To serve, lift from pan to cutting board and remove foil. Let stand at room temperature 10 minutes for easier slicing. Stand remaining topping pouch in boiling water to soften. Drizzle each slice with topping.

Makes 8 to 10 servings

Preparation Time: 15 minutes
Freezing Time: 4 hours

Peanut Butter Loaf

Pastel Swirl Dessert

A lovely dessert suitable for a shower, luncheon or any occasion!

     1 package (3 ounces) ladyfingers, split
  1⅓ cups boiling water
     2 packages (4-serving size) JELL-O® Brand Gelatin Dessert,
          any 2 different flavors
     1 cup cold water
        Ice cubes
     1 tub (12 ounces) COOL WHIP® Whipped Topping, thawed, divided

TRIM about 1 inch off 1 end of each ladyfinger; reserve trimmed ends. Place ladyfingers, cut ends down, around side of 9-inch springform pan.* Place trimmed ends on bottom of pan.

STIR ⅔ cup of the boiling water into each package of gelatin in separate medium bowls at least 2 minutes until completely dissolved. Mix cold water and ice cubes to make 2½ cups. Stir ½ of the ice water into each bowl until gelatin is slightly thickened. Remove any remaining ice.

GENTLY stir ½ of the whipped topping with wire whisk into each gelatin mixture until smooth. Refrigerate 20 to 30 minutes or until mixtures are very thick and will mound. Spoon mixtures alternately into prepared pan. Swirl with knife to marbleize.

REFRIGERATE 4 hours or until firm. Remove side of pan before slicing.   *Makes 16 servings*

*To prepare in 13×9-inch pan, do not trim ladyfingers. Line bottom of pan with ladyfingers. Continue as directed.

Preparation Time: 30 minutes
Refrigerating Time: 4½ hours

Pastel Swirl Dessert

Chocolate Swirl Cheesecake

1 package (11.1 ounces) JELL-O® No Bake Real Cheesecake
2 tablespoons sugar
⅓ cup butter or margarine
2 squares BAKER'S® Semi-Sweet Baking Chocolate
1½ cups cold milk, divided

MIX crumbs, sugar and melted butter thoroughly with fork in 9-inch pie plate until crumbs are well moistened. Press firmly against sides of pie plate first, using finger or large spoon to shape edge. Press remaining crumbs firmly onto bottom using measuring cup.

MICROWAVE chocolate and 2 tablespoons of the milk in microwavable bowl on HIGH 1½ minutes or until chocolate is almost melted. Stir until chocolate is completely melted.

BEAT remaining cold milk and filling mix with electric mixer on low speed until blended. Beat on medium speed 3 minutes. (Filling will be thick.) Spoon 2 cups of the filling into crust. Stir chocolate mixture into remaining filling.

SPOON over cheesecake. Cut through batter with knife several times for marble swirl effect. Refrigerate at least 1 hour. Garnish as desired. Store leftover cheesecake in refrigerator. *Makes 8 servings*

Preparation Time: 15 minutes
Refrigerating Time: 1 hour
Microwave Time: 1½ minutes

Creamy Lemon Bars

Luscious, lemony treats—perfect with an afternoon cup of tea or glass of milk.

1½ cups graham cracker crumbs
½ cup sugar, divided
½ cup (1 stick) butter or margarine, melted
1 package (8 ounces) PHILADELPHIA® Cream Cheese, softened
2 tablespoons milk
1 tub (8 ounces) COOL WHIP® Whipped Topping, thawed
1 package (4.3 ounces) JELL-O® Lemon Flavor Cook & Serve
 Pudding & Pie Filling *(not Instant)*
¾ cup sugar
3 cups water, divided
3 egg yolks

MIX crumbs, ¼ cup sugar and butter in 13×9-inch pan. Press firmly onto bottom of pan. Refrigerate until ready to fill.

BEAT cream cheese, remaining ¼ cup sugar and milk until smooth. Gently stir in ½ of the whipped topping. Spread evenly over crust.

STIR pudding mix, ¾ cup sugar, ½ cup water and egg yolks in medium saucepan. Stir in remaining 2½ cups water. Stirring constantly, cook on medium heat until mixture comes to full boil. Cool 5 minutes, stirring twice. Pour over cream cheese layer.

REFRIGERATE 4 hours or until set. Just before serving, spread remaining whipped topping over pudding.   *Makes 15 servings*

Preparation Time: 25 minutes
Refrigerating Time: 4 hours

White Chocolate Cheesecake

A truly luxurious dessert with a rich, silky texture.

> 1 package (11.1 ounces) JELL-O® No Bake Real Cheesecake
> ⅓ cup butter or margarine, melted
> 2 tablespoons sugar
> 1½ cups cold milk
> 1 package (6 squares) BAKER'S® Premium White Baking Chocolate Squares, melted
> 2 squares BAKER'S® Semi-Sweet Baking Chocolate, melted (optional)

MIX crumbs, butter and sugar thoroughly with fork in 9-inch pie plate until crumbs are well moistened. Press firmly against side of pie plate first, using finger or large spoon to shape edge. Press remaining crumbs firmly onto bottom of pie plate using measuring cup.

BEAT milk and filling mix with electric mixer on low speed until blended. Beat on medium speed 3 minutes. (Filling will be thick.) Reserve about 3 tablespoons melted white chocolate for garnish, if desired. Stir remaining melted white chocolate into filling mixture. Spoon into crust. Drizzle with reserved melted white chocolate and melted semi-sweet chocolate, if desired.

REFRIGERATE at least 1 hour, if desired.   *Makes 8 servings*

Preparation Time: 15 minutes
Refrigerating Time: 1 hour

Take the mystery out of making cheesecake with this recipe made extra simple with JELL-O No Bake Cheesecake.

White Chocolate Cheesecake

Tropical Terrine

A slice of this will magically transport you to a beach in the Caribbean.

  1 package (3 ounces) ladyfingers, split, divided
1½ cups boiling water
  1 package (8-serving size) or 2 packages (4-serving size) JELL-O®
    Brand Orange Flavor Sugar Free Low Calorie Gelatin Dessert
  1 can (8 ounces) crushed pineapple in juice, undrained
  1 cup cold water
  2 cups thawed COOL WHIP LITE® Whipped Topping
  1 can (11 ounces) mandarin orange segments, drained
    Additional thawed COOL WHIP LITE® Whipped Topping
    Kiwi slices
    Star fruit slices
    Pineapple leaves

LINE bottom and sides of 9×5-inch loaf pan with plastic wrap. Add enough ladyfingers, cut sides in, to fit evenly along all sides of pan.

STIR boiling water into gelatin in large bowl 2 minutes or until completely dissolved. Stir in pineapple with juice and cold water. Refrigerate 1¼ hours or until slightly thickened (consistency of unbeaten egg whites). Gently stir in 2 cups whipped topping and oranges. Spoon into prepared pan. Arrange remaining ladyfingers, cut sides down, evenly on top of gelatin mixture.

REFRIGERATE 3 hours or until firm. Place serving plate on top of pan. Invert, holding pan and plate together; shake gently to loosen. Carefully remove pan and plastic wrap. Garnish with additional whipped topping, fruit and pineapple leaves.   *Makes 12 servings*

Preparation Time: 30 minutes
Refrigerating Time: 4½ hours

COOL TIPS: *If you put a dab of shortening in the corners of the loaf pan, the plastic wrap will adhere to the pan more smoothly and easily. To keep its shape, leftover dessert can be returned to the loaf pan and refrigerated.*

JELL-O® Frozen No Bake Peanut Butter Cups

1 package (16.1 ounces) JELL-O® No Bake Peanut Butter Cup Dessert
⅓ cup melted margarine
1⅓ cups cold milk

PLACE topping pouch in large bowl of boiling water; set aside.

PREPARE crust mix as directed on package in medium bowl. Press onto bottoms of 12 to 15 foil-cup-lined muffin cups (about 1 heaping tablespoon per muffin cup).

PREPARE filling mix as directed on package in deep, medium bowl. Divide filling among muffin cups. Remove pouch from water. Knead pouch 60 seconds until fluid and no longer lumpy. Squeeze topping equally over cups.

FREEZE 2 hours or until firm. Store, covered, in freezer up to 2 weeks.

Makes 12 to 15 cups

JELL-O® Frozen No Bake Cookies & Creme Cups: *Prepare JELL-O® No Bake Cookies & Creme Dessert as directed on package, pressing prepared crust mix onto bottoms of 12 foil-cup-lined muffin cups. Divide prepared filling mixture among cups. Top with reserved cookies. Freeze and store as directed above.*

Preparation Time: 15 minutes plus freezing

Easy Eclair Dessert

This terrific dessert is a great crowd pleaser.

   27 whole graham crackers, halved
    3 cups cold milk
    2 packages (4-serving size) JELL-O® Vanilla Flavor Instant Pudding
        & Pie Filling
    1 tub (12 ounces) COOL WHIP® Whipped Topping, thawed
    1 container (16 ounces) ready-to-spread chocolate fudge frosting
        Strawberries

ARRANGE ⅓ of the crackers on bottom of 13×9-inch baking pan, breaking crackers to fit, if necessary.

POUR milk into large bowl. Add pudding mixes. Beat with wire whisk 2 minutes. Gently stir in whipped topping. Spread ½ of the pudding mixture over crackers. Place ½ of the remaining crackers over pudding; top with remaining pudding mixture and crackers.

REMOVE top and foil from frosting container. Microwave frosting in container on HIGH 1 minute or until pourable. Spread evenly over crackers.

REFRIGERATE 4 hours or overnight. Cut into squares to serve. Garnish with strawberries.   *Makes 18 servings*

Preparation Time: 20 minutes
Refrigerating Time: 4 hours

JELL-O Pudding is the perfect ingredient for making easy homemade desserts. To make this already delicious dessert even more decadent, try substituting chocolate graham crackers and chocolate pudding for the ones used above. This is any chocoholic's dream!

Easy Eclair Dessert

Holiday Specialties

Tropical Cake Squares

1½ cups boiling water
1 package (8-serving size) or 2 packages (4-serving size each)
   JELL-O® Brand Orange Flavor Gelatin
2 cups cold pineapple orange juice or orange juice
1 package (12 ounces) pound cake, cut into 10 to 12 slices
1 package (8 ounces) PHILADELPHIA® Cream Cheese, softened
¼ cup sugar
1 tub (8 ounces) COOL WHIP® Whipped Topping, thawed
2 cans (15¼ ounces each) fruit cocktail, drained

STIR boiling water into gelatin in large bowl at least 2 minutes until completely dissolved. Stir in cold juice. Refrigerate about 1½ hours or until thickened (spoon drawn through leaved definite impression). Meanwhile, line 13×9-inch pan with pound cake slices, filling any holes with cake pieces.

BEAT cream cheese and sugar in large bowl until smooth. Gently stir in whipped topping. Spread evenly over crust. Top with fruit. Spoon thickened gelatin over cream cheese layer and fruit.

REFRIGERATE 3 hours or until firm.   *Makes 15 servings*

Preparation Time: 15 minutes
Refrigerating Time: 4½ hours

Tropical Cake Square

Sparkling Dessert

1½ cups boiling water
1 package (8-serving size) or 2 packages (4-serving size) JELL-O®
    Brand Sparkling White Grape or Lemon Flavor Gelatin Dessert
2½ cups cold club soda or seltzer
1 cup sliced strawberries

STIR boiling water into gelatin in large bowl at least 2 minutes until completely dissolved. Refrigerate 15 minutes. Stir in cold club soda. Refrigerate 25 minutes or until slightly thickened.

SET aside ¾ cup thickened gelatin in medium bowl. Gently stir strawberries into remaining gelatin. Spon into champagne glasses, dessert dishes or 2-quart bowl. Beat reserved gelatin with electric mixer or high speed until fluffy and about double in volume. Spoon over gelatin in glasses or bowl. Cover.

REFRIGERATE 3 hours or until firm.   *Makes 8 to 10 servings*

Note: To prepare with champagne, use 1 cup cold champagne and 1½ cups cold club soda.

Preparation Time: 15 minutes
Refrigerating Time: 3¾ hours

Choose the best container for efficiency when making this recipe. Metal bowls chill more quickly than glass or plastic bowls so your gelatin will be firm in less time.

Sparkling Dessert

Graveyard Pudding Dessert

Even the ghosts will go for this!

3½ **cups cold milk**

2 **packages (4-serving size) JELL-O® Chocolate Flavor Instant Pudding & Pie Filling**

1 **tub (12 ounces) COOL WHIP® Whipped Topping, thawed**

1 **package (16 ounces) chocolate sandwich cookies, crushed**

Decorations: assorted rectangular-shaped sandwich cookies, decorator icings, candy corn and pumpkins

POUR milk into large bowl. Add pudding mixes. Beat with wire whisk or electric mixer on lowest speed 2 minutes or until blended. Gently stir in whipped topping and ½ of the crushed cookies. Spoon into 13×9-inch dish. Sprinkle with remaining crushed cookies.

REFRIGERATE 1 hour or until ready to serve. Decorate rectangular-shaped sandwich cookies with icings to make "tombstones." Stand tombstones on top of dessert with candies to resemble a graveyard.

Makes 15 servings

Preparation Time: 15 minutes
Refrigerating Time: 1 hour

JELL-O® Fun Facts

This recipe is a great one to remember when you are the person in charge of the school or team snack. It can easily be changed into a soccer or football field, hockey rink or any desired theme. Prepare as above and just garnish appropriately.

Graveyard Pudding Dessert

Ghoulish Punch

2 cups boiling water
1 package (8-serving size) or 2 packages (4-serving size) JELL-O®
    Brand Lime Flavor Gelatin Dessert
2 cups cold orange juice
1 liter cold seltzer
  Ice cubes
1 pint (2 cups) orange sherbet, slightly softened
1 orange, thinly sliced
1 lime, thinly sliced

STIR boiling water into gelatin in large bowl at least 2 minutes until completely dissolved. Stir in cold juice. Cool to room temperature.

JUST before serving, pour gelatin mixture into punch bowl. Add cold seltzer and ice cubes. Place scoops of sherbet and fruit slices in punch.

Makes 10 servings

Preparation Time: 15 minutes

JELL-O® Fun Facts

JELL-O Gelatin with its wide variety of fruit flavors makes an excellent base for easy and delicious drinks for a crowd.

Cranberry Apple Pie

Chopped apple and walnuts add delightful crunch to this irresistible pie suitable for any holiday gathering.

> 2 cups boiling water
> 1 package (8-serving size) or 2 packages (4-serving size) JELL-O®
>   Brand Cranberry Flavor Gelatin Dessert, or any red flavor
> ½ cup cold water
> ½ teaspoon ground cinnamon
> ⅛ teaspoon ground cloves
> ½ package (4 ounces) PHILADELPHIA® Cream Cheese, softened
> ¼ cup sugar
> ½ cup thawed COOL WHIP® Whipped Topping
> 1 prepared graham cracker crumb crust (6 ounces)
> 1 medium apple, chopped
> ½ cup chopped walnuts

STIR boiling water into gelatin in large bowl at least 2 minutes until completely dissolved. Stir in cold water and spices. Refrigerate about 1½ hours or until thickened (spoon drawn through leaves definite impression).

MEANWHILE, mix cream cheese and sugar in medium bowl with wire whisk until smooth. Gently stir in whipped topping. Spread onto bottom of crust. Refrigerate.

STIR apples and walnuts into thickened gelatin. Refrigerate 10 to 15 minutes or until mixture is very thick and will mound. Spoon over cream cheese layer.

REFRIGERATE 4 hours or until firm.   *Makes 8 servings*

Preparation Time: 20 minutes
Refrigerating Time: 5¾ hours

Double Layer Pumpkin Pie

It just wouldn't be Thanksgiving without this pie.

½ package (4 ounces) PHILADELPHIA® Cream Cheese, cubed, softened
1 tablespoon half-and-half or milk
1 tablespoon sugar
1 tub (8 ounces) COOL WHIP® Whipped Topping, thawed
1 prepared graham cracker crumb crust (6 ounces)
1 cup cold half-and-half or milk
2 packages (4-serving size) JELL-O® Vanilla Flavor Instant Pudding & Pie Filling
1 can (16 ounces) pumpkin
1 teaspoon ground cinnamon
½ teaspoon ground ginger
¼ teaspoon ground cloves

BEAT cream cheese, 1 tablespoon half-and-half and sugar in large bowl with wire whisk until smooth. Gently stir in 1½ cups whipped topping. Spread onto bottom of crust.

POUR 1 cup half-and-half into bowl. Add pudding mixes. Beat with wire whisk 1 minute. (Mixture will be thick.) Stir in pumpkin and spices with wire whisk until well blended. Spread over cream cheese layer.

REFRIGERATE 4 hours or until set. Garnish with remaining whipped topping and sprinkle with additional cinnamon.   *Makes 8 servings*

Double Layer Chocolate Pie: *Omit pumpkin and spices and increase half-and-half to 1½ cups. Prepare recipe as directed, substituting JELL-O Chocolate Flavor Instant Pudding for vanilla pudding.*

Preparation Time: 15 minutes
Refrigerating Time: 4 hours

Double Layer Pumpkin Pie

Quick-and-Easy Holiday Trifle

A festive trifle that takes but a trifling twenty minutes to make.

- **3 cups cold milk**
- **2 packages (4-serving size) JELL-O® Vanilla Flavor Instant Pudding & Pie Filling**
- **1 tub (8 ounces) COOL WHIP® Whipped Topping, thawed**
- **1 package (12 ounces) pound cake, cut into ½-inch cubes**
- **¼ cup orange juice**
- **2 cups sliced strawberries**

POUR milk into large bowl. Add pudding mixes. Beat with wire whisk 1 minute. Gently stir in 2 cups of the whipped topping.

ARRANGE ½ of the cake cubes in 3½-quart serving bowl. Drizzle with ½ of the orange juice. Spoon ½ of the pudding mixture over cake cubes. Top with strawberries. Layer with remaining cake cubes, orange juice and pudding mixture.

REFRIGERATE until ready to serve. Top with remaining whipped topping and garnish as desired. *Makes 12 servings*

Preparation Time: 20 minutes
Refrigerating Time: 1 hour

Quick-and-Easy Holiday Trifle

Layered Cranberry Cheesecake

Tangy cranberries and crunchy walnuts make this festive cheesecake extra special.

> 1 package (11.1 ounces) JELL-O® No Bake Real Cheesecake
> 2 tablespoons sugar
> ⅓ cup butter or margarine, melted
> 1½ cups cold milk
> ½ cup whole berry cranberry sauce
> ¼ cup chopped walnuts, toasted

MIX crumbs, sugar and butter thoroughly with fork in small bowl until crumbs are well moistened. Press firmly onto bottom of foil-lined 9-inch square pan.

BEAT milk and filling mix with electric mixer on low speed until well blended. Beat on medium speed 3 minutes. (Filling will be thick.) Spoon ½ of the filling over crust. Cover with cranberry sauce and walnuts. Top with remaining filling.

REFRIGERATE at least 1 hour. Garnish as desired.

Makes 9 servings

Preparation Time: 15 minutes
Refrigerating Time: 1 hour

Cheesecake dates back to the Roman Empire days and still remains one of the most popular desserts of all times.

Index

METRIC CONVERSION CHART

VOLUME MEASUREMENTS (dry)

1/8 teaspoon = 0.5 mL
1/4 teaspoon = 1 mL
1/2 teaspoon = 2 mL
3/4 teaspoon = 4 mL
1 teaspoon = 5 mL
1 tablespoon = 15 mL
2 tablespoons = 30 mL
1/4 cup = 60 mL
1/3 cup = 75 mL
1/2 cup = 125 mL
2/3 cup = 150 mL
3/4 cup = 175 mL
1 cup = 250 mL
2 cups = 1 pint = 500 mL
3 cups = 750 mL
4 cups = 1 quart = 1 L

VOLUME MEASUREMENTS (fluid)

1 fluid ounce (2 tablespoons) = 30 mL
4 fluid ounces (1/2 cup) = 125 mL
8 fluid ounces (1 cup) = 250 mL
12 fluid ounces (1 1/2 cups) = 375 mL
16 fluid ounces (2 cups) = 500 mL

WEIGHTS (mass)

1/2 ounce = 15 g
1 ounce = 30 g
3 ounces = 90 g
4 ounces = 120 g
8 ounces = 225 g
10 ounces = 285 g
12 ounces = 360 g
16 ounces = 1 pound = 450 g

DIMENSIONS

1/16 inch = 2 mm
1/8 inch = 3 mm
1/4 inch = 6 mm
1/2 inch = 1.5 cm
3/4 inch = 2 cm
1 inch = 2.5 cm

OVEN TEMPERATURES

250°F = 120°C
275°F = 140°C
300°F = 150°C
325°F = 160°C
350°F = 180°C
375°F = 190°C
400°F = 200°C
425°F = 220°C
450°F = 230°C

BAKING PAN SIZES

Utensil	Size in Inches/Quarts	Metric Volume	Size in Centimeters
Baking or Cake Pan (square or rectangular)	8×8×2	2 L	20×20×5
	9×9×2	2.5 L	23×23×5
	12×8×2	3 L	30×20×5
	13×9×2	3.5 L	33×23×5
Loaf Pan	8×4×3	1.5 L	20×10×7
	9×5×3	2 L	23×13×7
Round Layer Cake Pan	8×1½	1.2 L	20×4
	9×1½	1.5 L	23×4
Pie Plate	8×1¼	750 mL	20×3
	9×1¼	1 L	23×3
Baking Dish or Casserole	1 quart	1 L	—
	1½ quart	1.5 L	—
	2 quart	2 L	—

Notes